our future losses, and present mysteries examined with no preference or perfunctory reverence. Each time I read Stuart Ross's work I feel grateful, hopeful, reminded to lift my skeleton up and enjoy the abundant wonders the world holds.'
— Gillian Wigmore, author of *Orient*

'Stuart Ross doesn't hold back, happily for us. In letting his poems go where they want to go, sometimes by leaps and bounds, he reminds us that poetic rules are meant to be broken and that the results, in the hands of a skilful poet, can be moving, or amusing, or subversive, or exhilarating, or all of the above. His work brims with surprises. From start to finish, *The Sky Is a Sky in the Sky* is a delightful and thoroughly engaging book.'
— Charles North, author of *News, Poetry and Poplars: Poems/Selected Prose*

'[Ross] is one of the most wildly imaginative and innovative poets we have.... There isn't anyone writing poems in Canada who can do what Stuart Ross does.'
— Michael Dennis, *Today's book of poetry*

'The universality of grief – and our avoidance of it – has never been made more poignant than in *The Book of Grief and Hamburgers*. Part memoir, essay, confessional, and poetry, Ross's work affirms that to love in this world is to lose in this world. But his book is also an act of resistance. Our greatest armour in the face of mortality is our insistence to never forget the people we loved and to hold tight to the memories that define us. Through his profound meditation, Ross beautifully reminds us that, when it comes to our grief, we are never alone.'
— 2023 Trillium Book Award jury citation

# THE SKY IS A SKY IN THE SKY

STUART ROSS

COACH HOUSE BOOKS, TORONTO

first edition

Published with the generous assistance of the Canada Council for the Arts and the Ontario Arts Council. Coach House Books also acknowledges the support of the Government of Canada through the Canada Book Fund and the Government of Ontario through the Ontario Book Publishing Tax Credit.

LIBRARY AND ARCHIVES CANADA CATALOGUING IN PUBLICATION

Title: The sky is a sky in the sky / Stuart Ross.
Names: Ross, Stuart, 1959- author
Description: Poems.
Identifiers: Canadiana (print) 20240438337 | Canadiana (ebook) 20240438345 | ISBN 9781552454916 (softcover) | ISBN 9781770568310 (EPUB) | ISBN 9781770568327 (PDF)
Subjects: LCGFT: Experimental poetry. | LCGFT: Poetry.
Classification: LCC PS8585.O841 S59 2024 | DDC C811/.54—dc23

*The Sky Is a Sky in the Sky* is available as an ebook: ISBN 978 1 77056 831 0 (EPUB), ISBN 978 1 77056 832 7 (PDF)

Purchase of the print version of this book entitles you to a free digital copy. To claim your ebook of this title, please email sales@chbooks.com with proof of purchase. (Coach House Books reserves the right to terminate the free digital download offer at any time.)

*For Charlie Huisken*

*&*

*For Mark Laba and Steven Feldman*

*&*

*For Laurie Siblock*

# CONTENTS

## I: THE SKY

## II: IS A SKY

## III: IN THE SKY

*Whoever you are, what do you know?*
　　　　　　　　– Lisa Fishman, 'September 20 – 21, 2013'

*Come to the sick man's bedside, sun.*
　　　　　　　　　　　　　　– Marin Sorescu
　　　　　(trans. Adam J. Sorkin & Lidia Vanu), 'Someone'

*I opened the Venetian blind. There was Stuart Ross, holding up a copy of* The Watchtower.
　　　– George Bowering, 'I Opened the Venetian Blind'

# I

# THE SKY

# I LOVE POETRY

I hate poems that contain the word *mortal*, the word
*angel*, the word *liminal*, the word *beauty*, the word
*scent*. *Mortal coil* is particularly loathsome, though
*Eddie Coyle was mortal* is passable. I hate poems that
mention *Perseus, Heracles, Hephaestus, Infestus,
Hydrochlorixideus*, but I like *hideous, rancid,
gizmo*. Oh, *Orpheus* is okay if it's in a poem by Mark
Strand. *Eclogue* blech, *epilogue* pretty good. I hate
the word *ekphrastic* so much it makes me hate
ekphrastic poems, except for Ron Padgett's
'Joe Brainard's Painting "Bingo,"' the best
poem ever written. I met Joe once
to interview him and was delighted he had
never heard of Margaret Atwood. I hate
poems that contain the phrase *I love* unless
they are written by Lisa Jarnot, and I love Lisa
Jarnot's poem 'Lisa Jarnot.' I hate poems
that want to teach me something. Epigraphs
from Isaiah, Leviticus, and Dana Gioia are
non-starters. I once offered Alice Burdick,
Jaime Forsythe, and Lance La Rocque two
hundred bucks to start up a photocopied
mag of Nova Scotia poetry. Another time
I cut off part of my thumb with an X-acto
knife. I hate myself for loving poetry; I love myself
for hating poetry. I hate poems about poetry.

## LAST POEM

This is the last poem. I'm jogging alongside it, writing as fast as I can, but each time I stop to read what I've written, I can't read my goddamn handwriting. There will be no other poems. This is my last pair of running shoes. My laces came untied. But each time I stop to tie them, they assume the form of my handwriting. I can't make out a word. I look up from the ground, away from the confident weevils and ants. Away from the twitching corpse of a June bug and from a glistening piece of chewed-up bubble gum. The poem has gotten away. I jog, then walk. What I do is walk. I am in a delicatessen that closed thirty years ago. A guy with muscles bursting through his shirt winds his arm around and around. Like he's going to throw the baseball. But the baseball is his fist. He looks at me like the pastrami sandwich looks at the vegetarian. The poem writes me a letter. It hates similes. The muscle guy looks at me. A baseball looks at me. A pastrami sandwich looks at me. I am a vegetarian. A fist – from where? – connects with my jaw. I sail through the air, right out the window, like a cowboy hurled from a saloon into the muddy street. The poem writes me a letter. I sail. The window shatters. A cowboy lands in the mud. I, that cowboy, brush the mud from my pants, until I notice my hands are manatees. *Can manatees kill you? Are manatees friendly? Can you keep a manatee as a pet, teach it tricks?* These are the first questions asked by Ayesha and Fischbaum in Miss Leibovici's Grade 2 class when Miss Leibovici holds up a photo of the manatee. I write a postcard to the poem. But I can't decipher my handwriting, so I don't know what I've told the poem or what I've asked of it. I drop the postcard into a mailbox. The mailbox is red. It is filled with bread. It is a breadbox.

I am a biped. Each foot that punctuates each leg holds a shoe. These are my last shoes. I will have no future shoes. I look up from my untied laces. I say something aloud but don't understand a word. I debate which direction to run, but, dearest, what's a direction?

## THE REST OF THE DAY OF REST

If men and women were less ephemeral, a sparkling bridge
would barge and bustle into the lagoon of their ancient noggins.
Marco Polo's yawn was a total con, filling the streets
with tightly packed gravediggers. Is this really necessary?
Is this thick city a thing we can swim through?
Let me explain. Don't listen.
Blood has been found guilty; its offence:
mistrust of the pukey mirror. Behold our ineffable delicacy,
the garbage strewn across our yard. A cottage. A drowning.
A pair of lovers can be useful but noisy.
Not expecting things to make sense, I tried to survive
with the aid of boiled water and party favours. I scampered
upstairs to scramble eggs, beneath the frown
of an ash-speckled tapestry. Music has never existed.
It weighs so little! Chaos theory is just a theory. Heaven
is a demonstrable fact. Violence is a religion,
a way of addressing god. Behold the miracle
of waning interest. What would Johnny Rotten do?
Pluck nudie mags from the infinite spaces between his teeth,
his stockings held up by garter snakes. Research can research
anything. A quiet thing. A mockingbird.
Imitation is a slimy germ. We made our first million
babysitting. Then we swam into the future, a desert
of unsorted chipmunks. What do you call it?
A 'panopticon of chipmunks.'
You rise like a burnt-out sun from the huddle of terrible
storm clouds. But what is the price of a slice of white
bread, an aloof loaf of idiotic nouns that have, at last,
come into fashion?

## ALTERNATING LEG MOTION

It's amazing, those legs beneath me.
How do they decide which one goes first
and which next? How do they decide where
to carry my torso, my arms, my noggin?
'It's stupid when he calls it a noggin,'
they think. How do they decide which
streets to haunt? Or when they will limp?
Maybe they'll leap. Or fold me
into a deep chair from which I will
never rise. I write a letter to the editor
re alternating leg motion. My legs
demand a full retraction.

Soon I am lying in a simple pine box.
Shovelfuls of dirt land on my noggin.
'It's stupid when he calls it a noggin,'
they think. And then they start again:
one leg, then the other. My knees bump
against wood. One knee, then the other.
How do my legs choose which knee
to bend? Might one knee bend twice
in a row? I know we're not getting
anywhere. Therefore:

my flesh melts away, and soon I am
only bones. Each leg just bones.
My noggin's a skull. 'It's stupid
when he calls it a noggin,' they think.
My legs are the keynote speakers

at a conference on Intersectionality
in the Motion of Alternating Legs.
During the question period,
a young student in a wheelchair
asks why they don't move in unison,
'like my wheels,' she says, and demonstrates.
One leg is speechless. And then the other.

## HIBERNATION

A fox stood in the icy road,
each eye a tiny bonfire.
I held my palms close
for warmth. Cars wove
around us, spewing smoke
out their windows.
I couldn't tell who the fox
was thinking of but its ears
were so pointy they punctured
the frigid air, and a great hiss
flung me into a neighbour's bushes.
I lay there till spring.
I wondered if I still
had a job. I craved a variety
of small mammals, plus
nuts and some fruits.
A letter arrived, addressed to me.
I ripped it open with my teeth.
*This is to inform you*, it read,
*that the Beth Radom Temple*
*has accepted your application*
*for membership in the Shabbat*
*Poetry Club. Please bring*
*your pointy ears.*

## POEM AT SIXTY-ONE

*'There was a little silence.'*
*– Flann O'Brien,* The Dalkey Archive

I can't decide which of my feet
is best. I put neither forward.
There are so many people
floating around now. The clouds
are teeming. Music saturates
our bones. I open a letter.
It indicates that I contain
a skeleton. Put your ear
to my rib cage and listen.
Do you hear the voices of my family?

Dry leaves whirl around me. Snow
covers my shoulders. It melts. Oh regard
the magnificent kingfishers alighting
upon my brow. There is no reason
to shudder. Absorb the soft hug
of silence. Lift thy skeleton into the air.
The abundant wonders will never bumble.

*18 July 2020*

## EDUCATION

Hello, multitude of spindly insects
marching through my withered veins.
Sit down for tea, a croissant.
Let me read you some Peter Altenberg.

I have been waiting for friends like you.
Companionship is a shaky ladder
leading to an attic filled with hermit crabs.
Oh, can you help me with this crossword?

A 247-letter word meaning *suit of porridge*.
Come gather round this window:
yonder: beyond the creek: beyond the field:
Lipizzaners reenacting the Last Supper

for a scene in Jean Renoir's latest
posthumous film. Comrade insects,
the world teems with such miracles.
Teach me all you know.

## FILM FESTIVAL

A movie about two people. A movie about two can openers. A movie about death crawling through a supermarket. A movie about the tension between competing products. A movie about a wise turnip. A movie about silent music. A movie about books with no pages. A movie about a pill that erases memory. A movie about I can barely lift myself up out of this chair. A movie about a movie about exhaustion. A movie about walking into a wall. A movie about a porcupine that becomes sheriff in a small prairie town. A movie about an unfilled grave. A movie about dancing with my grandmother at my bar mitzvah. A movie about ashtrays. A movie about lining up at night, in the cold. A movie about noses.

## HANS ARP & OTHER MATTERS

I instructed my left eyeball
to read everything it could find
about how the Dadaists spent
their leisure time, and to my right eyeball,
I said, 'Watch out for that dark-haired
girl I loved in Grade 2, the one with
the flaring nostrils and the lavender
Hush Puppies, who once helped me up
when I tripped in the schoolyard, whose lips
turned bright red when she chewed
emergency gum, whose wild-haired mother
she hid from her classmates, and who,
for Halloween, dressed as Petunia the Duck.'
I hadn't seen her for forty-eight years,
and now she is a lawyer, a painter,
a scriptwriter, or living in Ptuj
with a new identity. I wanted only
to hear, once more, her voice, her
slight lisp; to gently touch her shining black hair
with just one of my seven-year-old fingertips;
I wanted to say I remembered her
and remind her of my name and the time
she cupped my elbow in her tiny palm
to help me to my feet as blood dribbled
from my knee and tears from my eyes,
including the one that, forty-eight years later,
would turn to me and say, 'Hans Arp
liked playing solitaire.'

## THE SKY IS A SKY IN THE SKY

*after Charles North's 'Day After Day the Storm Mounted.
Then It Dismounted'*

The sky dismounted and spent
the rest of its life on earth, occasionally
sliced by tornadoes and frightened
by the rumble of skyscrapers
herding their baby skyscrapers.
Some of us live in houses and some
beneath waterfalls, and mice
live anywhere their twitching
whiskers fit. The sky takes inventory
of the birds sailing through
what was once the sky: how many
had become dentists? florists? strippers?
umpires? coroners? A meadow of questions
billows toward the horizon and just
as I am about to respond
a set of tender fingers
rakes my thinning hair. A shadow
is the beard of an idea. An idea
is a doomed aspiration. That
tingling sensation in my pocket
is not chewed gum but a cluster
of stupid nouns that, joined at the hips,
creates a quivering language
uttered only by clouds.
A knock at the door.

It is Jack Teagarden, stars twinkling inside
his beautiful head. Come on in, Jack,
I'd like you to meet this tumbler of brandy.
Let's reminisce about Herald Square,
its magnificent mechanical clock.
As you walk, you walk through sky,
your voice throwing shadows like
misplaced notes into the Hudson River.
We are all particles, Jack. And soon we
weary, for we have wandered so far,
from Alberta to Albuquerque, where
deer and hornets wear sweaters
of steamed broccoli. *Our skin
acts as a protective wrapper*,
Jack says. And: *Lovely weather
we're having*.

## FIREBALL XL5 AUBADE

I pilot a ship, deke missiles, take
brutal abdominal strikes, nodes
waving in my stomach like
seaweed in that other Super-
marionation world, the one where
Marina plays Ladyfish to
Troy Tempest's Mr. Limpet.

Each night I return to Space City,
where I'm pumped full of morphine
and made to run through the same
room over and over like an actual
Flintstone. Every time I gaze
into your starry eyes, you draw
a small tick on your clipboard. At night,

the groans from the other beds
drift like ghosts through the hallways.
The air is sucked from my cabin, and
as I lie dying, I hear my mother cry,
*O Absalom my son, O Steve Zodiac,*
*O Stuart, O Zalman Nehemiah, O Seth,*
and I shrink into her warm arms

that no longer live, and yet still
she is my mother. The cat cries
to go out but it's way too cold.
I promise to decompose
quietly as I can manage.

## VALEDICTION

All that will
be left of me:

in the margins of books
pencilled murmurs

you will never
decipher.

## BOUNCING BALL

A guide appears in your living room, followed
by a cluster of tourists brandishing wooden spoons.
You sit in the old wing chair, reading a hardcover copy
of *Marjorie Morningstar*. The spirit of your dog
lies curled at your feet, doesn't even lift her adorable head
to greet the visitors. You ask these people
not to get fingerprints on your ceiling, not to clack
their spoons so much, please, not to draw swastikas
on synagogue walls, to help themselves to some fruit,
to maybe have a cup of tea, then never come back.
You tell the guide you are not a monument,
a historical plaque, a famous painting, a notable grave,
a landmark. You pull a couple of twenties
from your pocket and push them into his fist.
'I will never forget you,' you say. Outside,
the winter fires crackle. A northern cardinal
darts from the smoke, flourishes its wings,
swoops toward the lake, admires its own reflection.
The horizon undulates. The full moon bobs along it,
like the ball bouncing along song lyrics
in one of those old cartoons, a technique
invented in the 1920s by Max Fleischer.
You dog-ear your page in the book, pull on
your grandfather's galoshes, and hobble
after the moon, singing her perfect song,
becoming smaller and smaller yes smaller,
disappearing into the impossible luminosity of tomorrow.


*1 January 2020*

## VARIOUS WORDS BY STEPHEN BROCKWELL
## PLUS SOME OTHER WORDS

You found an eye in a flash of light,
a blur you wound around your neck
when the temperature plummeted.
You are, well, pretty concerned with
meaning and I know that meaning
is important and Niko the dog, gobbling
up a tub of Cheez Whiz, knows it,
too. Violas crow in the distance,
hammered and staggering like Frank Sinatra.
I attend the theatre in your head, which reclines
in leaves of grass as you peer into the moonglow above.

*Is it plastic-wrapped?* you ask. I say,
*Oh look, it's Parc Jerry Lewis!*
The guy in the engine room
wipes grease from his forehead
and pops a stick of gum in his mouth,
and another in yours. You
turn your head 360 degrees,
focus your zoom-lens eyes, perform
a miracle that offers comfort to those without
speech or dictionaries. I am a schlepper.
You are a Gordian knot in a bowl
of alphabet soup, dog-paddling
toward the magnificent tinted horizon.

## RAZOVSKY ON THE VOLGA

*for Gala Uzryutova*

The sun bobs on the surface
of the Volga River. It is pink.
It is blue. It is grey. Razovsky
sits at his piano on a rowboat
thirty metres from the shore.
The shore is speckled with seaweed.
Fog crawls along the water.

His piano teacher, Peterson,
looks like Tchaikovsky. Razovsky
has a wind-up Tchaikovsky
atop his piano. He hasn't
practised all week. He had toys
to play with, cartoons to watch.
His fingers stumble over the keys,
Volga boatmen, but he's thinking
of other things while he plays.
Guilt, but also guilt, and guilt.
For Peterson, this is torture.

A girl from a nearby village
watches from beneath a larch.
She sees this fisherman every summer.
He is so old. His arms so thin.
He pushes his oars through the fog, then drifts.
She thinks she hears him singing
but it's only the dirge of a herring gull riddled –

## 25 JULY 2020

A mask slides
all over my face
and shoulders.

*

The solid white line
dividing the lanes
is flaking.

*

Charles North reads
Nathanael West's
*The Day of Locus Solus.*

*

The lead in
my pencil keeps
break keep
keeps break
breaking.

*

That's not
chewed gum – it's
ants.

## PARIS

Where the Nith

and the Thames

intersect

Nelson's house

stands

empty.

## THE AIR, THE SKY

There are creatures in the walls. We hear them scurry and scratch,
gnaw on the insulation, tangle the wiring. At night they write poems
on tiny typewriters about how they hear creatures
outside the walls. They hear us use blenders, pencil sharpeners,
contraptions whose purpose they could never conceive of
and neither could we if no one had invented them. Another

thing there is is air. So much of it. You find it between
the leaves of poplars and in the tunnels beneath ant hills
and bobbing on ponds and rivers. Let's go breathe some air.
Let's paint a picture of it. If you don't get the angles right,
it doesn't judge you. The creatures in the walls
mistake *poplar* for *popular* but the *u* doesn't judge them.
Everything makes mistakes. I have made
twenty or twenty-one of them. Tom Clark
wrote a book called *Air*. Page 20 has
'A small / black worker ant / moving

diagonally' and page 21's got 'A moon in the
blue morning.' The moon is surrounded
by infinite sky, which we're connected to
by dollops of air.*

*1 January 2021*

* Perhaps if I wrote a book called *Sky*, I'd become more poplar.

## NEW YEAR'S EVE, 2020

The television fell off the shelf
and broke my head.

*


My legs got tangled
in the Blue Danube
when I came up for air.

*


The sky turned black
then white again
again.

*


My ship was made of paper.
I walked naked in the rain.

*


I stuck a shelf on the wall.
It fell and broke my head.

*

Garbage
slithers up
my pencil.

*

My ship is made of sand.
All I remember
about *Destination Gobi*
is Richard Widmark.

*

I stuck my broken head
on the shelf
I stuck on the wall.

*

A ribbon of melancholy
ties a melon to a collie.

# LIFE BEGINS WHEN YOU BEGIN THE BEGUINE

*for Charles North and Ron Padgett*

A pancake of snow slides down the side of the building.
It passes floor after floor. A pigeon and a blackbird
stop in midair to watch it but soon get bored.
Someday we will talk on the phone and see each other
like we are on TV. I'm not kidding. Someday
we will have a real television right in our own living room.
We will watch Jack Benny and Edith Piaf circle each other,
tense and masked. Plus there will be ads for cigarettes and bras.
Someday a rectangle with four wheels will carry us
wherever we want to go. At night, it will sleep in our 'driveway.'
Don't forget to put up the top! The sidewalk peers up,
sees a pancake of snow approaching. It experiences suspense.
I pronounce every word as if I am mouthless.
I keep all your letters in the credenza and end
all my letters with a cadenza. O beloved chunk
of geography, place Ljubljana in my backyard.
We can roar up and down the funicular.
Someday a stack of pages will become attached and
declared a book. As James Tate once said,
'My cuticles are a mess.' Inspired, I wrote
a Broadway musical about cuticles, choreographed
by Busby Berkeley. It closed after just one day
but changed the lives of those who saw it.
Look. Someday we'll understand each other. Someday
we will learn how to grieve. Just sit back and wait
for the pancake to hit the pavement.

*1 January 2022*

# II

# IS A SKY

## BIRD SNOW ON HARD TRACKS

*through Nelson Ball*

A yellow ice bird will soon turn
the red night mist into feathered mice

Grey days chatter and chirp among the falling rocks
A flurry of silence buttons the gently flowing air

The naked tree among cold January crickets
brings a yellow yellow yellow horizon

to the dead railway bridge beneath
a trace of blackened caterpillars

Cornstalks dart where the wind is obscured
by the present thick chaos that hyphens

hundreds of bent strands of future failures
I crawl through quiet brown November leaves

until Barbara whispers into my ears & my ears
swirl with the words & the words blossom

like skirts awaiting a band of red sunset
the ephemeral window of lightening morning

Here here here under the fallen yellow spruce
green birds rained on black birds, listening

to silent insistent words even when a cloud mother
leaves a perfect blue frost mat to fill cornfields

fill the lake air with pastoral grey sparrows
The forgotten bare trees twitch all evening

so anyone who swallows their winter words
will lose velvet speech – leave it in a yellow

yellow yellow night where snow shifts into fog
This pale remembrance will be a paper fire

the small birds touched en masse after the long winter
The Strohms' cold poems whisper to heavy branches

pointing restlessly at a hump of drooping friends
making the yellowish walnut moon hop on leathery thunder

and this snow darkens all the dead leaves
At dawn green red brown ochre reveals my little face

Wind falters like temporary trees – listens to
November grasses before small birds rattle the sunrise

but now the riverbank leaves fifty cold words near
stately ants and ties white paper across time

Every-rhyme snow soon bites chimney caterpillars
and our complementary blades of grey daylight fall

along the visible shift of time in indistinct words
falling down the little licey earth     But I hear eyes

I hear silent cold crickets gently approaching spring mud
All the pale trees fall in a river while devils paint

interstices of green morning snowdrops against large
unseen owls and intermittently I play twist the cornfield

until this flat day whispers in evening snow
This blue maple declined your dark hair and the whole

dark sky becomes fuzzy sunlight like mist tracks
on blue water while your arching fall branches come around

Silver sidewalk grasses surrounded by bright leaves
grow for hidden glimpses of sunny corn stalks outside

the sheltering car stirring in a grey winter coat or the yellow
of your distinctly false hair now delineating the daylight rain

Maple maple maple was the substance and seedling
the blue-grey disc from the lake's hard balance

Light settles over the small willow's very brown eyes
as clouds stand over spike of the painterly night

Owls hear a field of perfect white fog
Owls hear a previously cold winter sunset

The darkness tops all the cedars and rolls corn trees
faster than September poems and December snow

Each bright twig shifts back and forth five times in the long tall wind
Always your presence brightly arcs in this fire of October leaves

Wind leaves the morning train and brightens the sunrise continuum
with yellows and reds from trees and reeds upon the different
    black sun

Wind stopped overcast snow from leaving the white bird
and the bat in a different grey dust – crickets walk away briefly

from the five leaves I carried through the still cornfield
I touch the snow trees' warm dance with edge-on insistence

then water it and scatter river clouds tonight on old river breeze
The yew recedes in almost white primaries brushed by a glimpse

of rained grey land and Every Street
rustles like feet afraid of air

lit by maple snow     I play the river in winter
and presently it disappears in sun talk

I hear yellow leaves rise
I glimpse the seagull alive

light dark light dark almost light
Lightning's dance bends over grasses

hides the spring     sways from here to here
Grey mornings lighten and snow washes back

nothing no sky no earth     Still I stand not afraid above
the small green sky and step slowly from leaf to branch

Rain goes home to reflect the shape of winter light
Each overcast day goes to the cornfield     It's always

bright in the winter here by the sky river
The 8th grey leaf measures reds and yellows

A bat shines nicely     Birds fall fall fall en masse
from the yellow winter sky & the grass wouldn't

come dance on a white mat of snow today
Birds used me to talk to each other

not to the sun's veery cold light
A tall yew records time and wind

holds every sun owl back from sun wind
There are not October leaves here presently

Spring winds themselves are crossing a whiter spruce
and spruce stir reeds and they go low by park snow

Other days are not so sligh–
they lie there and talk all day

Come hear yellow's indivisible sound
Soon reds are offered more sky

It was all here on the leaf leaf leaf
Leaves hang a sign from some high tree

Dawn rushes through air wind air rain air sun
and now it steams cedar leaves now spruce

Cedar spruce grass pine
All others were mine

No air ever     slight air here
Sun will appear     day for fallen day

## RACTER IN THE FOREST

The white dog
stands

before

the black
cottage.

*

Walter Mondale
tilted his head:

the hum
of hounds
and of doves.

*

Ms. Otter
and Nelson Ball
chanted

about mansions
and trucks,
about phonographs.

*

I'll be right back,
Woody Woodpecker.

Okay,
I'm back.

*


A sane cat
is
a sober cat.

A soul
is contagious.

A cottage.
It's interesting.

*


Because bugs
are convinced.

## TALES OF FLISK, #18

In the early days of radio
constant mayhem entertained
those who tuned in to *Flecker
the Bumbling Mesmerist*,
whose star, Ritz Silverfarb,
soon earned enough
to give up his rocket ship
upholstering business. Big deal
when the show offered to
broadcast from the first town
that would change its name
to Flecker the Bumbling
Mesmerist, which Flisk,
British Columbia (last stop
before heading east
on the Salmo-Creston Pass), eagerly

did.

These days, the children of Flecker
the Bumbling Mesmerist
have no idea
who you're talking about
when you mention Ritz Silverfarb,
whose statue looms in front
of the town's post office,
nor can they name a single
episode of the radio show
that put their town on the map.

But old Mr. Snitchell,
who sits on his porch
awaiting a plate
of ham sandwiches
(no crusts)
prepared by his wife, Snooky,
who passed thirteen years ago –
why, he can spiel
every bit of dialogue

*(You want I should stack the chickens one on top of the other?)*

that ever entered
the ears of those

*(Who invited this tedious nudnik to our seder!)*

who crowded around
old radio sets

*(So I advised Mrs. Haftwurcel to adopt a ventriloquist dummy!)*

listening to the rollicking
adventures of Moishe Flecker

*(Soon we'll all be little flecks – just bupkis – in the void … )*

every Sunday evening
at seven. Then

suddenly

everything revolved around
hula hoops, and
a conscienceless wall
of crackling flames
razed the land.

*This*

*has been brought to you*
*by Snip Snip Woof Woof,*
*the most reliable*
*dog clippers in the galaxy.*
*Princey will lick your face*
*all day long as the*
*children look up*
*from their Etch A Sketches*
*and chuckle.*

## THE ANGLO-SAXONS. TAKE NINE.

Sometimes I sleep. I can barely feel it.
My tiny, stupid utterance is cast as a voice-over
during the credits of an epic film about the fifth-century
Anglo-Saxons who migrated, disguised in face shields,
into the empty British aisles of Sainsbury's,
where they scratched at Bingo cards
with their chewed-up fingernails.

I turn the camera toward my own face and I am shocked.
'Do you work in pediatrics?' I ask myself.
'I am paralyzed,' I say.
'I am stuffed,' I reply.
I am stuck in the mirror of my own awareness.
I admire my eyes. My eyes have changed. A change
is as good as a muscle

gone slack. Oh, tiny stupid utterance! That's no mirror.
It doesn't reflect nothing. It's a wall of lead blocking our view
of the distant horizon. The cheerful endpoint
of nuclear decay. I reach into my pocket for another mask. Then
I reach into my pocket for another mask. I forage for another mask
in my pocket. The pocket is located in pants, my trousers – no,
my slacks! I go slack.

## RAZOVSKY HAS SOMETHING TO SAY

Razovsky has never triumphed
on the esteemed grid
that serves as a battlefield
for tic-tac-toe, nor has he ever
won a game of chess, thoroughly
cooked an egg, painted all four walls
of a room (by the time he gets
to the fourth, years later,
the first has begun to fade and peel),
or finished reading a Tom Clancy novel.
He tosses his cigarettes to the sidewalk
half-smoked, and mould grows
on the surface of yesterday's coffee
that perches on the corner of his desk.

But when the kitchen table wobbles,
he produces a nearly empty matchbook
from his shirt pocket, tears off the cover,
folds it into a smaller square, and tucks this
under the table leg. Now the thing is steady.
He pulls on his heavy overcoat and
steps into the street. A bus rattles past him
on Wyandotte, rain leaks from the coughing
clouds, he has to keep lighting
his cigarette again. There's a sentence
he knows he needs to finish, he's had
seventy years, maybe a few more, he can
never remember. 'I want – I – How can I –
When will – Does she know what I – How
do you – When's the best time to – '

And then he is lifting into the air, past
the rooftops of buildings, past telephone wires,
and Mrs. Razovsky stops stirring
the mah jong tiles, the clacks give way
to a windy silence, and there –
she hears it again – that familiar cough
of the man who never finished anything,
who she once left for six weeks, who she taught,
in what were clearly her last days, how to choose
fresh produce, who promised her he'd take care
of their sons. She pulls herself to her feet
and can just make out his overcoat, gets a whiff
of his stinking cigarettes. She remembers then,
as her fingers touch his bristled cheek,
he has a sentence to finish.

## OPENING NIGHT

Who has launched the floating eggs? Those with degrees
in business or commerce. A tulip or some other
cannibalistic flower coughs into the fold of my sex an
opinion that bobs across the sweat of my ghastly forehead
until a cigarette's stranglehold steals his breath
and slams him to the kitchen floor. She cops to
having little left to gasp her declarations of love,
so she doesn't come home: she cradles a rabbit in the turret
of the tower she erected while sleeping, comforted
by the weight of Phyllis Diller's ebullient necklace,
summoning the march of nutcrackers through the resplendent
heft of the iron gate. Quality is what it's all about. An effusive holler
into the wizened ear of the man lying fetal on a sofa as Alzheimer's
puts on Broadway plays between his teeth and toes. Look there!
The light leaks out slowly beneath the splintered door.

## WILLOW STREET

*for and after Nelson Ball*

Nelson and I
sit facing
each other
in silence

I get up
put a kettle
on the two-
burner stove

sit back down
resume
our silence

the kettle
rattles
I pour us some tea

sit back down
resume
our silence

we cover
a lot
of ground


*15 August 2019*

## BILL GOT PISSED

Bill got pissed
when I mentioned
that book he wrote
with Jim
said how dare
you bring that up
why do you
torment me
I said I love
that book I had
no idea it would bug
you but Bill sliced me
from his life
        however I still
love it wish
it was back in
print and I wonder
what Jim would
think of that novel
now if he were
still alive and Bill is
dead now and
they are both dead
and I gently place
a copy of *Lucky*
*Darryl* in your lovely
trembling hands
that I adore

## BLATT

The gravel road
is my grandfather
hunched over
and shuffling ahead,
adjusting his dentures
every few steps,
squinting at the silhouette
of his sewing machine
at the top of the rise.
The sky is a sheet
of brown paper towel
on which he scrawled
some Hebrew letters
as he lay in hospital
unable to speak.
The soup in my bowl
is the puddle of memories
that flickered in his brain
as his breathing stopped.
The face in my mirror
is a thumb and thin forefinger
pushing a length of black thread
through the eye of a needle.
A steady cold breeze
slipping under the door
is the question
I never asked him.

## BLOOM

I crouched
in front
of my father's
grave

plunged
my fingers
into the dirt

grabbed him
by the necktie
pulled him up

pressed my face
to his
unshaven chin

## MATH & SCIENCE

*for Barry*

I was 35 when Mom died
at 66. 41 when Owen
died at 46. A tiny lull, then
(still) 41 when Dad died
at 76. Now I am 60,
Barry, & you are gone
4 days now at 69. For
19 years it was just us 2. We talked
on the phone 1 time a week.
988 times. Except 1 year
when we said 0 to each other.
So, that's 936. If we saw each
other 1 time a month,
except for those 12 after
we fought, that's 216 times
we saw 1 another
when it was just the 2 of us.

The final wisp of smoke
from your final cigarette
may still be perceivable among the clouds:
the precise composition of smoke
depends on the nature of the fuel,
the temperature of the flame,
& wherever the hell the wind is going
& whether it's in a hurry. Math
& science are ways

to not think about things
that are not
math & science.

## TINY CREATURES

*after 'Insects' by Chika Sagawa (trans. Sawako Nakayasu)*

Bugs are little things that fly in your mouth
when you shout or are agog. They create
little bugs through bug sex so fast
it would blind you.

You can trim the edges off this planet
like a slice of bread. Eat those
bumps of pus. Can you taste each
white blood cell, the cell's garbage
and diseased tissue?

At night, the city places its ball gown
on a rotisserie.

I fasten my flesh with clothespins to a rope.
I am made of shivering snakes.

I will not tell you what it is
that obscures my eyes and nose.

The absence of light is like birthday
candles for a woman whose skin, although
damaged, is intact. Her happy face,
which she shoplifted, spins,
spins, spins.

## THE MIST

I lie
in the
dark my
brother lies
in the ground
my father
mother they lie
in the ground oh
yeah my other
brother lies
in the ground
it's dark in
here they say

I am
a vegetarian
an insomniac a
sad sack and a
Jew with
bad posture and I
once saw Walter
Mondale (he was
pretty short) my
memory is
terrible and I crack
my knuckles my
favourite movie
is *the incredible*
*mr limpet* have

you ever
noticed the way
fish don't shop
for fish food

time scrapes
its rake
across my
face three
wise rabbis play
pinochle on
my grave the thing
about existing is
it never stops
you can always
drink the mist
that rises from
where your body
used to be

## A TOY BIRD

*with Clare Shaw*

A paper airplane hit me in the head.
I unfolded it: a catalogue of your crimes.

1. You did not leave the room as you found it.
2. There was glass on my carpet.

I thought I might never walk again.
Nothing about this speaks of love.

Boll weevils speak of love, as do flecks
of dust on a broken chandelier. We

have lips to keep our mouths shut,
to kiss and to get stuck to frozen fences.

There was wood where your tongue
should have been; I could not kiss you.

I looked away and when I looked back
you'd become a toy bird, hanging

from a string above my cluttered desk.
I loved you the more for it,

though I stopped believing in you.
Professor Feldstein said fondness is

measured in the contrails of ghosts
and ink smudged across diary pages.

I'm not sure what I make of that, but today
the wind is a ghost at the window

and the windows have all swung open
and my house is crowded

and though my feet are bloodied
I think that I understand. I could not kiss

your wooden tongue. The sun hid
in the clouds behind a mystery novel.

The cases of humans in my house
kept increasing. We bided our time

folding paper airplanes.

## SUFFICIENT EVIDENCE, OPUS 19

*after Barbara Guest's 'The Knight of Sun'*

My feathered enemies
lurk by the foaming flames,
their foreheads damp
in the winging breeze.
My thoughts are concave
like the ragged tooth trembling
in the archway of your pitiful gob.
The instruction manual
says I am a loser,
puffing in a monsoon of ginger ale
and shivering sand.

Night arrives.
It has curves
in all the right places.
Its language melts with the snow,
revealing creatures of armour
and sundry wacky farm critters.
I occupy my shiny hands,
rock like a leaf on a rock.
I gather sufficient evidence.
I give myself a tetanus shot.

> Next thing you know
> thin streams of light
> separate my toes.
> I give each a name.

## SELF-PORTRAIT

*after Joe Brainard*

CRISP
My hand is cold amid the celery.

BATH MAT
Everyone's feet turn to water.

MATHEMATICS
I don't add up.

FOLLOWER
You all buy potato chips after I.

DIVINITY
The finger in my right nostril heard confession from the finger
in my left.

ELBOW WAX
The coffee table slides beneath my arm.

WET TOWEL
Matters have become rather heavy.

WEEPING WILLOW
Where the trunk meets the ground I sit in sorrow.

WEATHER REPORT
I did not choose to fasten my puckered lips to the storm cloud.

FALLING
I fall, and pass the falling bird.

STATION WAGON
The ditch skids onto the highway, swaying.

PONY
I was never upon a pony.

WINDOW
My neighbour burns his toast.

NO SCHOOL
Various sick cheeses skated across my broken Etch A Sketch.

DEAD TREE
The leaves fill my cheeks.

CHINESE FOOD
Everyone pass everything at once, but slowly.

## RESURRECTION

*'Today I am practicing animal stares.'*
*'It's an air ballet for migrating birds.'*
*'We owe it a resurrection.'*
*– Dag T. Straumsvåg*

I reach into the sky and pluck two stars.
I jam them in my face for eyes.
A fox and a Gestetner walk by and shrug.
Today I am practicing animal stares.

On the stove, the sauce is bubbling over.
The cat quit her subscription to *Debt Quarterly*.
The house rises up past the telephone wires.
It's an air ballet for migrating birds.

The election results are indeterminate.
Every child is entitled to gum.
Judy Garland's portrait falls to the floor.
We owe it a resurrection.

## POEM FOR SUNDAY (JANUARY 1, 2023)

On the first day, I woke in the dark.
The wind howled,
rattling my windows and eyeballs.
I invented the electric light
and turned it on. Another me
appeared on the floor,
like a crime-scene outline
drawn in black chalk. I introduced
myself and invited him
for dinner. He had never tried
Chinese food, so that's what we ordered.
My doorbell rang. Bags appeared.
We arranged the cartons on the table.
My shadow said so much
depends on the egg rolls
drizzled in plum sauce
beside the orange chicken.
I thwacked him on the head
but my hand went right through him.

This is a poem about tragedy.
I'll start again.
I dreamed I was visiting
Opal and Ellen Nations,
and we ordered Chinese food.
Because it was New Year's Day,
the food took so long to arrive that
Opal kept eating slices of bread
with Cheez Whiz while Ellen

showed me the linoleum tiles
she'd chosen for the kitchen floor.
Nothing is more or less interesting
than when someone shares
their dream with you. Suddenly,
a shard of sun sneaks between
the curtains and enters my eyeballs.
I inflate. I drift out the window
and into the morning-lit sky.
It's all so beauti–
                    I deflate
and plummet to the ground.
A pebble is lodged in my shoe.
The breeze ruffles my dwindling
hair. The shadow of my hand
caresses my unshaven cheek.
We people on the pavement
looked at me. Everything I've said here
is remarkable. A burst of the present
plunges into your outstretched arms.


*1 January 2023*

## ONE DAY IN 2023

*for Laurie*

it's 2023 and we're all flying around with
jetpacks strapped to our backs, holy cow
we gotta get somewhere, that place
we gotta get to but you can't even
see the sky so many goddamn people
flying around with their jetpacks
going wherever the hell they're going
– really, you have to fly above
everyone else to even get a glimpse
of the empty sky and everyone tries
to fly above everyone else, we're like
a cloud of aphids like a stampede
after a football game like
infinite leapfrog

down on the ground
a terrier, maybe
a bichon frise
sniffs at a fire hydrant
circles it a few times
lifts his leg
and as god is my witness
out streams a sparkling
ray of sunlight
and lo we are saved

## LIST&NING

*for Extended Music Collective*

A splutter
of smoke

knocks gently
on the basement
door

as the house
creaks
in pleasure.

*for Obsidiana Duo*

A tiny bird
leans
on a piano.

A song
escapes
its beak.

The bird
chases it.

*for Neuro Trash*

The beige
sandwich
crosses
the room

and punches
the green
wall. 'I can't

stop
thinking
of you.'


*for Noise Catalogue & Else, if Else & Extended Music Collective*

Each rainbow
fell
at its own
speed.

The river
received them
in its cool
flowing
arms.

*for Iida-Vilhelmiina Sinivalo & David Potvin*

The heart
stretches
through
the night.

It stretches.

Look: it
stretches.

# III

# IN THE SKY

## THE BREATHTAKING ARRIVAL OF KAY FRANCIS
## INTO MY LIFE

*after and in memory of Bob Hogg (who is not the 'you')*

When I
rammed god
down your
throat you
gagged, then
sucker-punched
me in the
solar plexus.
We went to
see *Trouble*
*in Paradise* (Ernst
Lubitsch, 1932)
and I couldn't
stop thinking
about Kay
Francis, daughter
of Katharine Clinton
and Joseph
Sprague Gibbs,
and who left
her millions to
seeing eye
dogs across
the nation.
We agreed
we were

changed men
and bought
a crumbling
parking lot
on the outskirts
of Kitchener and
built a monument
to friendship
made of popsicle
sticks (the monument,
not the friendship)
and there we
gathered to
worship each
time we lost
a body part,
until we were
little but
ether colliding
every Friday
at 8 p.m. as
the Shabbos
candles flickered
and guttered and
Kay Francis
drifted overhead,
her hair
the unending
waves of the
Atlantic Ocean,
and said, 'The
important thing

is to lie
a lot and
to the right
people.' A slab
of sunlight
crawled across
the distant
mountains,
spotlighting
a couple of
graceful brown
rabbits leaping
like rabbis
across a
shimmering
auditorium
of undulating
wheat,
bringing every-
thing into
focus.

## POEM FOR CATRINA LONGMUIR

Two nails extend from the wall beside my bed. The paint
on the wall is textured, like a rough fabric. Flakes of paint
erupt where the nails extrude. As if they are trying to hold
the nails in. The paint on the wall is grey, or a blue, or

a mottled green. Like my father, I bluff at colours. From
each nail a thin shadow extends horizontally to the right.
To the left of the nail on the left, and up, a shadow mass
begins from the corner of an unfolded piece of paper lying

on a stack of books on my night table. The shadow
mass continues down and to the right, just missing the nail,
veering diagonally down, passing four inches below
the nail on the right, with a couple of sharp drops, like

a New Mexico horizon. My friend Richard died in
New Mexico. The unfolded paper is a photocopy of
a tender poem he wrote at twenty, based on a photograph
of himself, his sister, and his brother. Richard's poem ends:

'Let the wind blow / You couldn't stop it if you tried.'
The nails supported your painting, Catrina,
for nearly a decade.

## MY IDEAS, MY FLOOR, MY MOTHER

I drank a small coffee each morning, nothing more. That was my only routine, according to the profile of me in the November issue of *Compound Blister*. The pendulous brain of my dream world would knock the empty espresso cup off the table. Upon the espresso cup is a photograph of my mother's face positioned within a light bulb, underneath which a manufacturer has installed the words 'You Light Up My Life' in a barely legible pink script. I busy myself. In my head I visit my mother's grave. In the distance, a black squirrel leaps like a cartoon ball bouncing along the lyrics of 'Don't Sit Under the Apple Tree with Anyone Else But Me.' There are not enough hours in the day, not enough days in the week, not enough staples in the centrefold. We do not always proclaim loudly the most important thing we have to say. That's what Walter Benjamin told me. I told him that I watched seven YouTube videos to determine how to pronounce his name and each pronunciation was different. I pick up the espresso cup and place it in the sink. My mother descends into the soapy water, her ideas intact. When the reporter calls, I tell her my brain is located in my head, which is located in my kitchen. She asks me where I get my ideas. She asks me what project I'm working on right now. She asks me which I like best: Formula One racing or Luis Buñuel movies. Then she holds up a hand, palm facing me, dirty fingernails facing her. 'Forgive me,' she says, 'I approach too many questions.' It is true that to ask is to approach, to become nearer, even to loom. I tell her I have a story to tell her. All of her becomes ears, and she articulates the transformation. I was tired, I said. I hadn't slept in four days. My vision was blurry and I was remembering things that hadn't happened to me. I climbed into my car, a bright red Dodge Housefly. I drove through the thick stench of night, sparks licking my windshield. The manual for my car cowered in the glove compartment, alongside six dead AAA batteries and a small card on which was printed the mourner's kaddish in Hebrew. A filament irritated my car's tires.

## MEMO

A man died
before his shadow.
And his shadow
went home, put a bullet
through his head. And
the tragedy is this:

the ambiguity
of the pronoun
*his*, and of the
adverb *before*.

It's like
we can no longer
communicate.

## SIX HOURS

In my dream, my dad went missing. His parking spot was empty, except for a puddle of oil. The police didn't take me seriously. I screamed at them over the phone. In my dream, Nelson Ball was a goat. We sat in his kitchen, wearing sweaters. He couldn't talk but he nodded a lot, he smiled. In my dream, my mother was on the phone, telling me where to find the cutlery. The drawer kept vanishing. In my dream, I was looking for a vegan restaurant in Pompano Beach. The restaurant was called Contingency Plan. A cool breeze blew in through the window. The night was busier than I'd expected. The shadows on the ceiling bided their time in the dark.

## MAY 14, 1980 (RÍO SUMPUL)

Why does the little girl cling to her father's long hair as he swims?

Why does the river's surface pucker when it's not even raining?

Who threw the babies into the air?

Everything quakes. The ground, the water, the clouds.

Why does a river have only two banks? Why not three? Four?

How come the earth erupts from the ground?

Why does the woman tie the babies to her body with her bra strap?

How strong are her arms?

How do you stop a baby from screaming?

How long will the copters hover above the shimmering blanket
  of black?

What is that quiet that comes from the depths?

The stones that riddle the banks are skulls.

The town is so far away. Was there a town?

Can six hundred truths rise up from the waters?

A memory escapes: a fluke: it hides in the woods.

## JENNY HOLZER

*for Kenn Enns*

Kennedy, you have
words in your brain
and words surround
you and you buy words
and say words and soon
you will have words on you.
Actual words right on you.
Jenny Holzer was born in
Gallipolis, Ohio, on July
29, 1950. Kennedy, inked
you will move through
public spaces. When you
reach Gallipolis, you will
light up and blink.

## WISEBERG PLAYS WITH HER GRANDSONS

Blatt sits at his black
contraption, foot pumping
the treadle, fingertips guiding
the grey fabric through, a hem
appearing like a grimace at night.
Nina is in the family room, her
inky eyes looking down
on her grandson's head, her
grandson pushing blocks across the floor,
red and yellow sedans speeding
over the carpet's vast desert.
The other grandson sits, too, on
the floor, his face just inches from
the TV screen, a black-and-white
clown peering back at him, their
noses almost touching. Nina
knows she may never see the third
grandchild: depends on her tumour's
schedule.
           The smiles that illuminate
her quiet face are brief and beatific.
It's a relief to sit here with these
children, or with her other daughter's,
the girls, or with her other daughter's,
the girls and their brother the prince.
Because otherwise she is back in her thirties
in the thirties, pressed with Blatt to the radio,
listening to the crematorium smoke,
the howls of those who disappeared,

who boarded airless boxcars,
somewhere in the somewhere of somewhere
across the ocean. And Blatt spits
on the side of his fist and erases
the white chalk line he'd traced
on the fabric. So many Blatts
and Wisebergs have vanished,
but these fine grey pants have hems.

## MICHAEL'S OFFICE

*in memory of Michael Dennis*

In Michael's office, we are surrounded
by poetry. Each passing month,
the space for books expands while
the space for people contracts. You feel
the poems on your clothes, your skin,
on your tongue. It is paradise.

Michael rolls a joint, turns up
the Coltrane. He sits at his desk,
while I am sunk in the chair across
from him, the most comfortable spot
on earth. To my left, out the window,
Michael and Kirsty's backyard, filled with
green and the colours of flowers.

I know nothing about flowers,
what any of those flowers are,
but I'm sure Michael could
identify each one. This is just
the smallest part of his wisdom.

## CHICAGO

*in memory of Richard Huttel*

the foamy water
reaches
now
to the cold
blue sky

Richard
sat here too
on this wood bench
saw this too

now he is ash
in the grass
in tree bark

and in my hair
I hope

## PROPOFOL

Nelson, no thinner
than usual,
lay in the hospital
bed, his
last word,
*Cold*, as
the propofol
flowed.

My last words
to Nelson
as I left
the room: *Goodbye,*
*Nelson.*

But he
was already
writing

his most
minimal poems.

## TAFFY AND CLYTEMNESTRA

*with Sarah Burgoyne*

It must have been magic or myth:
I saw only part of my face in the mirror.
I recognized myself the moment they washed up
onto the shores of my consciousness
with their twenty combined toes.
But I needed an answer when I stepped out to see,
spray-painted across my cracked windshield:
'This is not my life.' Ah yes, I think I remember.
Couldn't eat. Couldn't write. Couldn't sleep.
My unanswerable sadness began because I
always confused her with her. Thing is,
modern oracles are so rare, they write
their names in a cloud of wet ink.
Someone told me they could be found
pulling taffy from the cashier's red hair.
When I ran into them, I sneezed
and the scent instantly triggered my memory.
She and she spent ten good years writing
an entire book of poems dedicated to
the abandoned lilies that close at night.
She pushed open her one good eye
with an answer as big as the hieroglyphic sea.
I asked her and her – the gentle catastrophe:
was it a small island or large one I saw,
maybe a decade ago? They cringed, juggling
small coffees squeezed in styrofoam cups.
She and she gazed into the linoleum horizon,

mouths bent in the shape of disappointment
because they'd never killed anything,
having met over a brown plastic tray.
Even in the absence of wind,
talking was difficult. She said it should be
called 'climbing.' Leaning forward,
she poured it from the dark cafeteria
into the damp web of questions.

## THE DOT WAS RED

In 1992, I read how I could put a dot
somewhere I looked a lot, and every time
I looked at that dot, I would remember to –

I worked at Harlequin Enterprises then,
copy-editing romance novels. I lived in a tiny
cubicle there, and I had a phone and I had
a computer, and I put a little sticker
in the form of a red dot on my phone.
I must have seen that dot several hundred
times a day, and every time I saw it,
I remembered to –

If you would like further information about
my tenure at Harlequin Enterprises, you can
reference an old poem of mine called 'Around
the Building,' in which I talk about things that
really happened and also things I made up.

One thing I really liked about that job
was bumping into Glenda at the subway station
where we both waited for the same bus. Glenda
worked across the road for a record company.
Plus she wrote songs and played guitar and
she shared some of those songs with me.
Glenda had red hair. We once went to see
*Kiss of the Spider Woman* together. When we stepped
off the bus, Glenda went to her building,
and I went to mine, where the first thing

I saw when I reached my cubicle
was the red dot. Immediately
I was reminded to –

One guy we worked with had a party in his apartment.
He invited us all to come. He didn't have any food or drinks
for his guests. There was half a chocolate cupcake
in his fridge and he ate it. I went out to the store and
bought two big bags of potato chips. I resented that
he didn't reimburse me for them. At one point,
some of us were out on his balcony and he was inside,
vacuuming his living room.

At Harlequin, I edited two hundred books about
love and about killing. The love books were
Temptations, Romances, Historicals, Suspenses,
Desires; the books about killing were Mack Bolan,
The Executioner, Deathlands. I developed
Crushes on three women at Harlequin and
wanted to kill one man. I watched the York
Mills bus pass by every twenty minutes
on the street below. The dot
on my phone was red.

## TEN

i.

I crawl along the beach
I turn transparent
a plant eats me
the ants applaud

ii.

the refrigerator contained only a rock
said where do you want to go?
how many flapjacks
received electroshock therapy
from Jean-Paul Sartre?

iii.

nineteen pickles arranged themselves
in the path
of a pockmarked Howitzer

iv.

I slithered down the silver railroad
a chunk of Appalachia
hung off the crusty mucus

I danced with Jacqueline Onassis
after the assassination
of her husband Burt Lancaster
in the party room
of our collective forehead


v.

I talk into a microphone
a microphone talks into a pancreas
a pancreas talks into a Frost fence
a Frost fence talks into the ear of Robert Frost
Robert Frost punches Stephen Crane in the face
Stephen Crane knocks over Hart Crane
on his way down


vi.

in the absence of a suitable chair
I sit on a blanket of swarming red ants


vii.

a part of me never wants to
leave a part of me
lying in the gutter playing pinochle
with a cotton boll weevil
named Sylvia

viii.

cutting a person's head in half
is best when the person is half-dead
you will learn so many things
o the swirls of the brain
o the cross-section of the skull
the little wiggling tip of the spine
(see one?) is our future
our temperamental orgasm


ix.

don't look at me
when I'm talking to you


x.

when she opened her eyes
a piece of bereavement
fell from one socket
*that looks like an ice cube* someone said
others of us thought it looked
more like the adjustable wrench
I used to rip my nose
from the centre of my face
as a way of becoming
more famous

## ITINERARY

I was riding backwards on a train
when I started to roar, and I roared
till my brow erupted in flames,
and everyone on the train
roared with me.
                When I woke (or maybe
when I slept), I was splayed in a
rust-covered tub of swampy water,
reeds poking out around my
spindly octopus. I mean corpus. I
tried to let out another roar
to see if the rust would roar
with me, but my efforts were
feckless, devoid of feck, feck-free.
What did, however, transpire
was this: A flock of delicate poodlejays
descended from the skylight above,
their feathery coifs (I'd thought
at first they were yarmulkes) rustling
as the birds circled the tub.
                  The poodle-
jay clearly in charge landed upon
my bony, blistered knee and proceeded
to declaim on a topic I found obscure,
the pith of which appeared to be
that I was dead. This thing of being
in a rusty tub in a dank, magnificent house
I only now realized I had never seen before:
this was death.

A frisson of ecstasy,
though it might have been grief, navigated
my shattered spine, and the poodlejays
roared, and I roared with them, and my train
thundered into its final destination.

## CAN'T EXPLAIN POEM

*after Lisa Jarnot's 'Tell Me Poem'*

I can't explain cartoons
that feature dolphins then I can't
explain why I constantly check
if my headlights are on and
my stove is off plus I can't
explain your poetry my
actions the concept of grief
the shape of my mother's
face so I walk along the sidewalk
and wait for someone to walk
along the sidewalk alongside
me carrying a broken umbrella
or maybe a paper bag of snap
peas plus an extra head for
when the first one gets tired
and a trail of cartoon animals
both black and white and
colour struggling to keep up
with the science of the brain

## AND THUS SHALL IT UNFOLD

You and I, we will spread a yellow blanket
across the green grass, and from our picnic basket
we will arrange a variety of cheeses, soft and hard,
and you will remember glasses, so we will pour
ourselves some wine, and we will sit cross-legged
facing each other's faces. 'Look!' you will murmur,
pointing to the sky, and there will hang
a magnificent canvas of birds, flapping in unison,
a giant arrow pointing south.
                                But instead of grass
there will be pebbles, small and hard like tumours;
instead of cheeses, corroded batteries and spark plugs;
instead of birds there will be the ashes of burning trees;
instead of wine, our sweat; instead of faces, dead bees.

## COOKERY

I put a stockpot on the stove,
pulled a chair up close.
The punk band in my bathroom
played their new album
with plungers and razors. The audience
leapt to their feet. I confessed
to the stockpot that I had failed.
Everything I had ever attempted
wasted everyone's time.
The flushing of the toilet
was magnificent. The Heaving Bedbugs
had vanished. 'Maybe,' said the stockpot,
'they left you an autographed poster.'
I switched on the stove,
rested my chin between
two burners. The stockpot began
to tremble and soon exhaled
a fat ribbon of smoke. That was
the first time I had played guitar.
I actually wasn't too bad. I went
to the cemetery where my parents
now lived. I carefully placed
the stockpot atop their roof.
'They'd be so proud of you,'
said the stockpot. I pulled up a chair,
straightened my crooked yarmulke.
And so began the post-punk era.

## TEA TIME

My nose becomes bored with the rest of my face.
It tugs in that direction and this, then manages
to crawl across my left cheek, down the side of my neck,
onto my shoulder where it leaps to freedom. Embarrassed
by the empty plain of my face, I stay home. I hide
in the attic and stumble on a copy of Gogol. I open to
a random page and an ant crawls out and onto my wrist,
up my arm, my shoulder, my neck, over my chin and
onto my face. My arm and throat tickle as a trail of ants
follows its leader, gathering in the bags beneath my eyes.

There they set up a Utopian society, a model for the rest
of the planet. They call it Undulating Mass Nation. My
friends call me Ant-Nose. I do the talk-show circuit,
and when the public tires of me, I am relegated to a circus
side show. Thirty years pass. When I die the ants leave,
disgusted. I lie in my coffin, unable to smell my own
decomposition. Each day I expect to hear a scampering
of nostrils on my grave, my nose come back to join me.
But all I hear is the rattle of a rusted kettle, telling me
my tea is finally ready.

## RAZOVSKY IN PARADISE

In the dark, Razovsky settles into his seat.
Around him: whispers, the crumpling of wrappers,
the scraping of feet. Music shakes the floor,
and the screen explodes in a burst of lightning.
Burt Lancaster, wearing only swimming trunks,
presses his sinewy body against a door as rain
pounds the terrible suburbs. He wraps his arms
around his naked chest and sobs. Razovsky
didn't sleep so well last night. He rubs his eyes,
then watches as Deborah Kerr walks slowly down
a long hallway illuminated by the sputtering
candle she holds before her. Her lips tremble
as she braces for the cries of ghosts, of children
possessed by the devil. Razovsky sinks further
into his seat and pats his shirt pocket for
cigarettes. Nothing. Terence Stamp stands over
the motionless body of Samantha Eggar,
his dark eyes empty of emotion. He thought
she'd come to love him. Outside the cinema,
on the sidewalk, Razovsky has forgotten
it's still afternoon. The sun pries open
his squinting eyes with a shoehorn
his grandfather brought from Russia.
Elizabeth Taylor comes to visit Montgomery
Clift in his tiny jail cell. She says she will
always love him and he marches off
to the chair. Razovsky shoulders through
the door of a cigar store, buys a Coke
and cigarettes from a guy in a yarmulke.

It's someone's yahrzeit tonight
but Razovsky can't recall whose.
He buys a candle. He'll remember later.
He pops open the Coke cap on a newspaper
box, takes a big gulp, and lights a Rothman's.
Kim Novak stands in front of the painting
of Carlotta Valdes. She's just left some flowers
on the dead woman's grave and now she's come
to the gallery to gaze at her portrait. Razovsky
regards the yahrzeit candle in his hand.
The soundtrack swells and the candle
turns into a ship. It's dark in the hold,
just a few dim light bulbs swing gently,
and Razovsky strains to see all
the faces, tired, pale, unwashed,
and he hears whispers, quiet laughter,
soft weeping. Soon he opens his eyes.
A child whips by him on a bike. Playing
cards slap in the spokes. Someone waves
from a station wagon. A weeping willow
sings like Enrico Caruso. A doorknob
appears in Razovsky's hand. He turns it.

## SONG

*for Cameron Anstee*

The bird
in
my ear

is a bird
in
the wall

is a bird
in
the air
in
a tree.

# I WASN'T REALLY PREPARED FOR ANY OF THIS

*for Pete McCormack*

For the blue-green fog that permeated my brain, the glacier
in my glass of Coke, the dog that quoted Heraclitus,
the book whose vowels blinked on and off
like a Broadway sign. I wasn't really prepared.
The wind that blew the river away, the tree
that took my car for a joy ride, the cartoon duck
that bore my voice, the executioner's winsome smile
and endearing cowlick, the burlesque dancer
in my cereal bowl. I confess: I simply wasn't
ready. For the library filled to the ceiling with
bright-eyed dolls' heads and expressionless
war criminals, I came unprepared. And just
as I opened my suitcase and looked for clean
socks, I reached for my nose, found empty clothes.

# SEVEN SLEEPS FOR A NEW YEAR

i.

When I wake
It will be the first day
Of something new
That tiptoes along a telephone wire
Catching fragments of conversation
And writing them down


ii.

I was snoring
My leg was in a weird position
It remembered a joke about a calf who mooed
But it was a leg calf


iii.

My teeth were grinding
My enemies
Into something
I could live with

iv.

The brownshirts chase me up the stairs
Soon I have no more floors to escape to
I shove open my eyes
Reach toward the night table
Sip some water
The brownshirts screech to a halt
They mutter
Scratch their heads
(One head per brownshirt)


v.

I yawn while sleeping
My stomach growls while I eat
I write a poem while someone reads one of my poems


vi.

The digital clock
Beside the glass of water
On my night table
Throws a red 3:26
Across my still face
The spider dangling
Above my head
Double-checks its watches

vii.

I was sleeping
I was not a hummingbird
I was not a can opener
I was not a wisp of campfire smoke
My head lay on a pillow
And a dream snuck out of my skull
Curled itself into a ball
Went bouncing off the walls
And out the window
Into the dark sky
Into the cold night
Into the broken world
Where it fixed everything


*1 January 2024*

## POEM

I see a light

at the end

of the tunnel

and beyond that

a tunnel

## NOTES

'I Love Poetry' – Jaime, Alice, and Lance never took me up on the mag money. Bruce LaBruce came to the hospital with me when I lopped off a thumb wedge.

'Last Poem,' 'Travel,' 'Opening Night,' 'The Anglo-Saxons. Take Nine.,' 'Racter in the Forest,' 'My Ideas, My Floor, My Mother,' and 'Ten' – Written in Sarah Burgoyne's Poetry Studio. Thanks, Sarah! 'The Anglo-Saxons. Take Nine.' is loosely based on a rough draft by André Babyn.

'The Rest of the Day of Rest' – Written during an online River of Words session with Toronto writers Heather Birrell and Rami Schandall. I don't recall what our source texts were.

'Fireball XL5 Aubade' – The 1962–63 TV series *Fireball XL5* was among the first to employ AP Films' revolutionary Super-marionation technique. Colonel Steve Zodiac commanded the vessel. Marina and Troy Tempest were characters in the 1964 series *Stingray*, which was set in 2046. Ladyfish and Mr. Limpet were characters in Arthur Lubin's 1964 partly animated film *The Incredible Mr. Limpet. The Flintstones* aired from 1960 to 1966. This was clearly an influential period in my life.

'Various Words by Stephen Brockwell Plus Some Other Words' – Borrows at times from the lines of superb Ottawa poet Stephen Brockwell. I think I wrote it for his birthday.

'Paris' – Nelson Ball's home at 31 Willow Street in Paris, Ontario, is being converted to condos, last I heard.

'Bird Snow on Hard Tracks' – Assembled using all the words from Nelson Ball's quietly magnificent collection *Bird Tracks On Hard Snow* (ECW Press, 1994), including dedications and titles. I occasionally took liberties in capitalizing and lowercasing words. And in using spaces mid-line in place of a period; Nelson did that only in a few early poems. Dashes are the only punctuation I brought from that book to my poem. Nelson got to see the first half (more or less) of 'Bird Snow on Hard Tracks' before his death on August 16, 2019. He seemed amused in his quiet way.

'Bill Got Pissed' – Although Bill Knott came to despise me for posting about it, I still treasure *Lucky Daryl* (S O M E, 1977), the collaborative novel he wrote with James Tate.

'A Toy Bird' – Written collaboratively with UK poet Clare Shaw for our virtual 2020 reading in the ink sweat & tears series at the Butchery, hosted by Martin Figura and Helen Ivory.

'List&Ning' – These tiny poems of gratitude were composed during a concert on 4 August 2023 in the Music & Sound Building at the Banff Centre for Arts & Creativity, in Banff, Alberta.

'Poem for Catrina Longmuir' – Catrina and I have been scheming to collaborate for over a decade. I keep a painting by her beside my bed to keep the plan in mind. The folded poem by Chicago poet Richard Huttel was handed to me by either his brother or sister at the celebration of his life. Catrina created the gorgeous cover for my novel *Pockets*.

'May 14, 1980 (Río Sumpul)' – Some three hundred to seven hundred Salvadoran refugees were massacred by Salvadoran forces in Río Sumpul as they attempted to flee to neighbouring Honduras. The Honduran military was complicit. The US Embassy in Tegucigalpa initially denied that a massacre had taken place, but eventually admitted that 'something happened.'

'Jenny Holzer' – Alludes to Ron Padgett's 'THE ELECTRIC EEL' from his poem 'Three Animals' (*Tulsa Kid*, Z Press, 1979).

'Taffy and Clytemnestra' – Written collaboratively with Montreal poet Sarah Burgoyne, for what occasion I do not recall.

## ACKNOWLEDGEMENTS

Some of the poems in this collection have made previous appearances, often in slightly or wildly different form. Gratitude to the editors of these publications. • 'The Sky Is a Sky in the Sky' in *Aphros* (2024) • 'Fireball XL5 Aubade,' Hibernation,' 'Can't Explain Poem,' and 'Hans Arp & Other Matters' in *Periodicities* (2024) • 'Opening Night' and 'Tales of Flisk, #18' in *Gargoyle* (2024) • 'Racter in the Forest' and 'Film Festival' in *The Minute Review* (2024) • 'Doppelgänger' and 'Poem' in *STUMPT* (2024) • 'Poem' in *NOON: journal of the short poem* (2024) • 'I Wasn't Really Prepared for Any of This' as a leaflet from Proper Tales Press (2024) • 'List&Ning' as a chapbook from Proper Tales Press (2023) • 'Bill Got Pissed' in *Peter F. Yacht Club* (2023) • 'Bird Snow on Hard Tracks' as a chapbook from above/ground press (2023) • 'Last Poem' in *Hamilton Arts & Letters* (2022) • 'Education' as a leaflet from Proper Tales Press (2022) • 'Resurrection' in *Cypress Journal* (2021) • 'Ten' as a PDF chapbook from Model Press (2021) • 'Poem for Catrina Longmuir' in *Poems for Reading*, by Dale Tracy (Deictic Press, 2020) • 'Can't Explain Poem' in the leaflet *Almonte* from Proper Tales Press (2019) • 'May 14, 1980 (Rio Sumpul)' in *Everyone, El Salvador* (Underline Studio, 2017)

I have dreamed of having a book with Coach House since I first visited the press at age fifteen, when Joe Rosenblatt brought my creative writing class there from the Alternative & Independent Study Program (my high school). A half-century wasn't too long a wait! Thank you to my kind and lively editor, Nasser Hussain; my very dear friend and hero and publisher, Alana Wilcox; Coach House champs James Lindsay and Crystal Sikma; and everyone else at Coach House, including the undersung crew in printing and binding. Gratitude to three writers I admire deeply: Charles North, Lisa Fishman, and Gillian Wigmore; I sure am moved by your generous words about this book. And to my comrade Nadine Faraj, what a cover painting you created for the front of this book! To collaborators Clare Shaw and Sarah Burgoyne, such fine poets, working with you enriched me. To my cousin Bev Bocknek, for straightening me out on family history. Thanks, as well, to my generous Patreon supporters. Finally, thank you – always – to Laurie Siblock.

**Stuart Ross** has published over twenty books of fiction, poetry, and personal essays, as well as scores of chapbooks. His most recent books are the memoir *The Book of Grief and Hamburgers*, winner of the 2023 Trillium Book Award, and the short story collection *I Am Claude François and You Are a Bathtub*. His latest poetry publications are the full-length collection *Motel of the Opposable Thumbs* and the chapbook *A Very Little Street*. Stuart received the 2019 Harbourfront Festival Prize, the 2017 Canadian Jewish Literary Award for Poetry, and the 2010 Relit Award for Short Fiction. He has been writer in residence at Queen's University and the University of Ottawa, has mentored at the Banff Centre for the Arts, and teaches Intro to Poetry at the University of Toronto School of Continuing Studies. For the past two years, Stuart has been collaborating with Montreal artist Nadine Faraj on paintings with text. His poetry has been translated into Nynorsk, French, Spanish, Russian, Slovene, and Estonian. Stuart lives in Cobourg, Ontario.

## SELECTED OTHER POETRY BY STUART ROSS

*70 Kippers: The Dagmar Poems*, w/ Michael Dennis, Cobourg: Proper Tales Press, 2020

*Sos una sola persona*, trans. Tomás Downey & Sarah Moses, Buenos Aires: Socios Fundadores, 2020

*Ninety Tiny Poems*, Ottawa: above/ground press, 2019

*Motel of the Opposable Thumbs*, Vancouver: Anvil Press, 2019

*Espesantes*, above/ground press, 2018

*A Sparrow Came Down Resplendent,* Hamilton: Wolsak & Wynn, 2016

*A Hamburger in a Gallery,* Montreal: DC Books, 2015

*Our Days in Vaudeville: Collaborative Poems*, Toronto: Mansfield Press, 2013

*You Exist. Details Follow.*, Anvil Press, 2012

*Dead Cars in Managua*, DC Books, 2008

*I Cut My Finger*, Anvil Press, 2007

*Hey, Crumbling Balcony! Poems New & Selected,* Toronto: ECW Press, 2003

*Razovsky at Peace*, ECW Press, 2001

*Farmer Gloomy's New Hybrid*, ECW Press, 1999

*The Inspiration Cha-Cha*, ECW Press, 1996

Typeset in Arno and Bourton.

Printed at the Coach House on bpNichol Lane in Toronto, Ontario, on Zephyr Antique Laid paper, which was manufactured, acid-free, in Saint-Jérôme, Quebec, from second-growth forests. This book was printed with vegetable-based ink on a 1973 Heidelberg KORD offset litho press. Its pages were folded on a Baumfolder, gathered by hand, bound on a Sulby Auto-Minabinda, and trimmed on a Polar single-knife cutter.

Coach House is located in Toronto, which is on the traditional territory of many nations, including the Mississaugas of the Credit, the Anishnabeg, the Chippewa, the Haudenosaunee, and the Wendat peoples, and is now home to many diverse First Nations, Inuit, and Métis peoples. We acknowledge that Toronto is covered by Treaty 13 with the Mississaugas of the Credit. We are grateful to live and work on this land.

Edited by Nasser Hussain
Cover and interior design by Crystal Sikma
Cover art: *A Solution*, by Nadine Faraj, 2024, watercolour on Arches paper.
    15 x 11 inches (detail); Photography credit: Michael Flomen
Author photo by Laurie Siblock

Coach House Books
80 bpNichol Lane
Toronto ON M5S 3J4
Canada

mail@chbooks.com
www.chbooks.com